AF673289

SMART BRAIN RIGHT BRAIN

An Introduction to Life Sciences

Om KIDZ
An imprint of Om Books International

First Published in 2021 by

Om Kidz | Om Books International

Corporate & Editorial Office
A-12, Sector 64, Noida 201 301
Uttar Pradesh, India
Phone: +91 120 477 4100
Email: editorial@ombooks.com
Website: www.ombooksinternational.com

Sales Office
107, Ansari Road, Darya Ganj
New Delhi 110 002, India
Phone: +91 11 4000 9000
Email: sales@ombooks.com

© Om Books International 2021
Author: Shweta Sinha
Editor: Kirti Pathak
Art & Design: Anshuman Pandey, Gaurav Bhandari, Harish Arya

ISBN: 978-93-5276-830-1

Printed in India

10 9 8 7 6 5 4 3 2 1

ALL RIGHTS RESERVED. No part of this book may be reproduced or transmitted in any form by any means, electronic or mechanical, including photocopying and recording, or by any information storage and retrieval system, except as may be expressly permitted in writing by the publisher.

CONTENTS

1. Living and Non-living Things	4
2. The Animal Kingdom	14
3. The Plant Kingdom	20
Let's Get Active	28
Glossary	32
Answers	32

1. Living and Non-living Things

This is a big rock.

This is Lisa.

Which of the two is a living thing?

Lisa's grandmother has told her that anything that breathes, eats and grows is a living thing.

Which of them does all these things and which one does not? Let us see...

Does Lisa breathe?

Yes, Lisa breathes in fresh air through her nose.

POCKET FACT

Every year, you grow taller by about the width of your palm.

Does Lisa eat?

Yes, Lisa eats. She loves ice cream.

Does Lisa grow?

Yes, Look at her growth chart.

Lisa **breathes**,
eats and **grows**.
She is a living thing.

POCKET FACT

Your baby pictures show how much you have grown since you were a baby, till now.

Does the rock breathe?
No.

Does the rock eat?
No.

Does it grow?
No.

The rock does not breathe, eat and grow. So it is not a living thing. What is a rock then? The rock is a non-living thing.

POCKET FACT

A river is a non-living thing. It moves and seems to grow but does not eat or breathe.

This is Lisa's puppy, Tim.

Is Tim a living thing too?

Does Tim breathe?
Yes, Tim breathes through its shiny, black nose.

Does Tim grow?
Yes, Tim will soon grow into a big dog.

Does Tim eat?

Yes, Tim gobbles up all the special dog food.
Tim is also a living thing.

POCKET FACT

Puppies grow very quickly. Most puppies grow into full-sized dogs by their second birthday.

This is Lisa's book.

Is the book a living thing or a non-living thing?

Does it breathe?
No.
Does it eat?
No.
Does it grow?
No.
This book is a non-living thing.

DID YOU KNOW?

Paper is made from plants. Sometimes, used paper is also recycled into new paper.

How many living things can you find in the picture?

How many non-living things can you find in the picture?

POCKET FACT

Non-living things cannot see, hear or feel anything.

2. The Animal Kingdom

Are all animals living things just like Lisa's puppy? Let us see.

Do animals breathe? Yes, animals breathe. You can see their bellies go up and down as they breathe.

Do animals eat? Yes, animals eat. Monkeys love bananas. Cows eat grass.

Do animals grow? Yes, animals grow too.

A lamb grows to become a sheep.

POCKET FACT

A baby lion is called a cub.
A baby kangaroo is called a joey.
A baby duck is called a duckling.
A baby cat is called a kitten.
A baby horse is called a foal.

Animals need air, water and food to stay alive. Animals grow and move. And yes, animals do one more thing like humans–they make babies that look like them. So, animals are **Living Things.**

Different kinds of animals

Some animals are big.
Some animals are small.
Some animals fly.
Some animals walk and run.
Some animals swim.
Animals are of different shapes, sizes and colours.

POCKET FACT

There are thousands of animals in the world that we know nothing about yet.

DID YOU KNOW?

The blue whale is the largest animal in the world. It lives in the ocean.

Animal Groups

All these animal groups make up the animal kingdom:

Mammals, like Dogs and Cats

Reptiles, like Lizards and Snakes

Birds, like Eagles and Parrots

Fish, like Sharks and Sea Horses

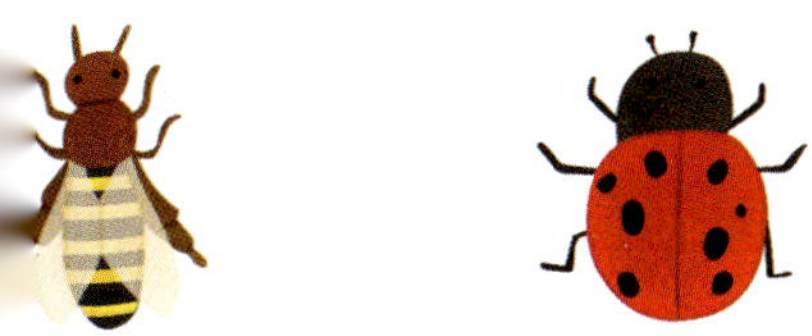

Insects, like Honeybees and Ladybugs

Mammals give birth to young ones. Reptiles, birds, fish and insects lay eggs.

POCKET FACT

Dinosaurs were giant reptiles that lived on Earth millions of years ago.

Body covering of different animals

Different animal groups have different types of body coverings.

DID YOU KNOW?

A dolphin looks like a fish but it is a mammal.

POCKET FACT

You and I are Humans. Humans are Mammals.

Mammals have hair or fur.

Reptiles have a dry skin or hard scales.

Only birds have feathers.

DID YOU KNOW?

Most birds fly. But the Ostrich and Kiwi cannot fly though they are birds.

Insects are small animals with a hard body covering.

POCKET FACT

Amphibians are animals that live on land and in water. A frog is an amphibian.

Fish have scales to protect them.

3. The Plant Kingdom

Look at the trees and plants outside. There are hundreds and thousands of plants and trees around us.

DID YOU KNOW? Some plants grow underwater on the seabed.

Some plants are as tiny as a small grain of rice. Some trees are bigger than a building with twenty storeys.

POCKET FACT

The redwoods are the tallest trees in the world. They grow in California, USA.

Let's Find Out! Are plants and trees living things?

Pull out a small plant from the soil.
Leave it around for a day.

What do you see?

The leaves begin to droop.
The plant dies.

Why did the plant die?

Plants take minerals and water from the soil. This is their food. Out of the soil the plant cannot get nourishment.
The plant dies.

So, plants are living things because they too require food to grow and remain healthy.

Do plants breathe?

Yes, plants do breathe. But where are their noses? Plants do not have noses. Their leaves do the breathing.

Do plants grow?

Take a seed, like the seed from a lemon or a bean. Wash the seed and plant it in the soil. Water the seed lightly every day.

POCKET FACT

The main parts of a plant are Roots, Stem and Leaves.

What happens?

A tiny plant begins to grow out of the soil. If you take good care of it, the baby plant, or sapling, will soon grow into a bigger one. Plants grow.

DID YOU KNOW?

The Methuselah is a pine tree in California, USA that is 4,000 years old.

Do plants make babies?

Where did your baby plant come from?
It came from the seed.
Where did the seed come from?
The seed came from a fruit.
Where did the fruit come from?
It came from a tree or a plant.
So, trees make the fruit.
Fruits have seeds.
Baby plants come from the seeds.
Trees and plants make babies.
So, trees and plants are also living things.

POCKET FACT

Some plants do not need soil to grow. They gather water and nutrients from the air.

Types of Plants

All plants are not the same size. Some are small and some are tall. Plants can be put into groups by their sizes:

Herbs are really small plants. They have a soft, delicate stem. Cilantro and basil are herbs.

Shrubs are bigger than herbs but smaller than trees. They are bushy. They have a woody stem. A rose bush and a lemon plant are shrubs.

DID YOU KNOW? Mushrooms may look like plants but they are not plants.

Creepers have such a soft stem that they cannot even stand. They creep on the ground. Pumpkin and watermelon plants are creepers.

Climbers are like creepers. They have thin, weak stems that cannot stand upright. But they have tendrils that help them climb. Grapevines and pea plants are climbers.

Trees are the most majestic of all. They are big and mighty. They have a thick woody stem called a trunk. Teak and mango are trees.

POCKET FACT

Some trees shed their leaves during winter. Other trees stay evergreen all year round.

Living or Non-living?

Tick the correct box.

	Living Thing	Non-living Thing
	☐	☐
	☐	☐
	☐	☐
	☐	☐
	☐	☐

Can you guess the correct animal group?

Tick the correct box.

Animals	Mammal	Reptile	Bird	Fish	Insect

Match the animals to their baby animals:

Match the pictures with the correct word.

Ball

Sun

Bird

Tree

GLOSSARY

Breathe	to take in air through the nose
Body covering	something that covers the body, so as to protect or conceal
Feather	one of the flat slender growths that cover the bodies of birds
Gill	an organ for breathing on an underwater creature
Grow	to become larger in size
Growth chart	a chart to measure size at different stages
Life science	the study of living organisms
Recycle	to reuse waste material by converting it into something new
Scales	an outer protective layer made up of flat, rigid, overlapping plate

ANSWERS

Page 28.

Page 29.

Page 30.

Page 31.